Functional Reactive Programming
Modernizing the Paradigm

Table of Contents

Chapter 1. Introduction

Welcome to our Special Report: "Functional Reactive Programming: Modernizing the Paradigm." This is an exploration of the ever-evolving world of programming, curated for professionals and enthusiasts alike who wish to stay abreast of influential trends. With the objective of unpicking the intricacies of Functional Reactive Programming (FRP), our report delves into its concepts, benefits, applications, and the significant role it carries in modernizing traditional methods. No need for apprehension; we've ensured to trod a courteous path through the technicalities, serving the facts in an easily digestible format. By the time you close our report, you'll comprehend why FRP is more than a trend; it's a revolution in the programming landscape. Be it out of curiosity or the hunger for knowledge, this report will prove a commendable investment. Let's together embark on this journey through the riveting world of FRP.

Chapter 2. An Introduction to Functional Reactive Programming

To frame the discussion in perspective, let's take a step back to cast our attention to traditional approaches to software development. Historically, programmers have orchestrated the flow of data in programs imperatively, which essentially means providing detailed step-by-step instructions for the computational tasks. However, as the complexity of software grew, and with the blossoming of multi-threaded and asynchronous tasks, this model began to show its cracks. A new paradigm was needed to manage the surfeit of interdependency without losing control over the flow and transformation of data.

Enter Functional Reactive Programming.

2.1. What is Functional Reactive Programming?

Functional Reactive Programming (FRP) is a paradigm for software development that integrates principles of functional programming (FP) and reactive programming. It's an approach where software systems are constructed by composing mathematical functions and maintaining reactiveness by continually responding to changes.

In essence, FRP emphasizes the use of pure functions (functions that do not cause side effects), and the application of these functions on multiple values over time. This distinction is crucial as it highlights FRP's superiority in handling time-varying or event-driven asynchronous data streams — a common occurrence in many modern software systems, especially in the front-end development and data analytics spaces.

2.2. The Backbone: Functional Programming and Reactive Programming

To understand Functional Reactive Programming, it's essential to dissect its roots: Functional Programming (FP) and Reactive Programming.

1. Functional Programming: It's a style of programming where computations are treated as mathematical functions. In FP, these functions are executed to produce results, not based on the program state and data change, but purely through the argument values.

2. Reactive Programming: On the flip side, reactive programming caters to applications with asynchronous data streams, focusing on the propagation of change. It is about building non-blocking, event-driven applications that scale seamlessly.

Together, these elements form the basis of FRP. The fusion of the principled construction from FP, and non-blocking asynchronous data handling from reactive programming, gives birth to an efficient and reliable programming model that gracefully balances precision and scale.

2.3. A Deeper Dive into Principles

FRP comes with a suite of singular principles that sets it apart from other approaches. Let's take a closer look at them.

1. Data Stream and Propagation of Change: In FRP, we conceptualize everything as a data stream. Whether it's variables, user inputs,

properties, caches, or data structures, they all are treated as a stream of data. This modality allows a declarative approach to operations, where we specify what needs to be done, not how to do it.

2. Observers: Observers operate on a pull-pull model. They listen for changes in observables and execute instructions based on these changes.

3. Schedulers: Schedulers provide a control point to programmers, dictating when and how tasks are executed in regards to concurrency and priority.

4. Disposables: Detailed and disciplined resource management is crucial in functional reactive programming. Disposables can be thought of as a contract, providing a link between system resources and observers, and helping manage the lifecycle of resources.

2.4. Advantages of FRP

FRP offers numerous benefits, especially for complex and highly interactive applications.

1. Declarative Code: FRP enables us to write declarative code, or, what we want to do rather than how we want to do it. This leads to more readable, maintainable code.

2. Efficient Resource Management: With disposables, resources can be cleaned up in a deterministic manner ensuring minimum memory leaks and efficient resource utilization.

3. Superior Error Handling: Through the propagation of errors as data through streams, and the ability to catch and handle these errors at composition boundaries.

4. Comprehensive Processing of Asynchronous Data: The FRP paradigm provides robust facilities for dealing with asynchronous and time-variant behaviors.

2.5. Rolling Up the Sleeves: Applications of FRP

The use of FRP can be found across a wide array of domains, including but not limited to- GUIs, robotic control systems, music synthesis, and others which have both asynchronous events and time-varying values. In the world of web and mobile app development, frameworks like React.js, Elm, and Redux thrive on the principles of functional reactive programming. Furthermore, in real-time data analytics, event stream processing frameworks such as Apache Flink also adopt the FRP style for stream processing.

2.6. Future of FRP

As software complexity continues to launch into unseen territories, the importance and applicability of FRP will only proliferate. Programs must handle data proficiently and react to events responsibly to handle the data-intensive applications of tomorrow, and FRP is pretty well geared to usher in that future.

In conclusion, Functional Reactive Programming is not just a buzzword. It's a remarkable technique assuring a fresh perspective to designing software applications. It arms programmers with powerful, reusable components that accelerate the development process and deliver more reliable, scalable programs. And for those with an appetite for evolving paradigms and practices, FRP is truly a savory feast. Discover its world, and it may well transform your approach to programming.

Chapter 3. Foundational Concepts and Building Blocks

As we initiate the discourse on Functional Reactive Programming, it is crucial to grasp the foundational concepts that make up this dynamic paradigm. These concepts are not entirely peculiar to FRP. Still, their interplay within the framework establishes a unique programming environment that facilitates elegance, safety, and the expressiveness of coding, especially in systems with discrete and continuous changes. So brace yourself for an in-depth analysis of these concepts, their intricacies, and the building blocks necessary for proficiently navigating the FRP landscape.

3.1. Function Purity and Referential Transparency

The foundation of FRP is rooted in functional programming (FP), thus inheriting the principles of function purity and referential transparency. Pure functions are those that, given the same input, always return the same output, and produce no side-effects. This property enables easy reasoning about the code, as it eradicates the concerns associated with shared mutable states.

Referential transparency, a feature of pure functions, dictates that an expression can be replaced with its corresponding output without altering the application's behavior. This allows for powerful optimization techniques like memoization, where function calls with the same arguments can bypass computation in favor of stored results.

Together, function purity and referential transparency guarantee the predictability and testability of code written in an FRP style, fostering robust software design.

3.2. Declarative Programming Model

FRP adopts a style known as declarative programming, which focuses on what the program should accomplish, rather than detailing how to achieve it. This abstracts the control flow and allows developers to articulate complex system behaviors concisely.

In contrast, imperative programming mandates an exact sequence of statements to alter the program state, limiting its expressiveness. By incorporating time-varying values explicitly and enabling their manipulation like any other variable, FRP provides an intuitive model for structuring such systems.

3.3. Immutable Data

Immutability is another vital characteristic of FRP that is borrowed from FP. Every value is unmodifiable once created. This means that rather than changing existing data, new data is produced. This trait eliminates the issues stemming from shared mutable state, offering additional safety and simplifying multi-threaded and concurrent programming.

3.4. Time-Varying Values: Behaviours and Events

Understanding FRP necessitates understanding behaviors and events, which give us a handle on dynamic, time-varying values.

Behaviors represent values that vary continuously over time. They abstract time-dependent values into a coherent model, making mental visualizations of changing states simpler. For instance, the position of a video game character is a Behavior—it is changing continually as the game progresses.

Events represent sequences of discrete occurrences. They are time-stamped values arriving asynchronously, like user inputs or web responses. They exhibit discontinuous changes, which are spaced apart.

These concepts, coupled with FRP's combinators (functions for combining behaviors and events), allow for expressing complex temporal interactions in a high-level, declarative manner.

3.5. Reactivity

FRP's distinctness is its inherent support for reactive systems, namely systems that react to changes over time or events. This is especially important in areas like GUIs, animations, robotics, and anywhere else where the system needs to respond promptly to external events, such as user input or sensor output.

In a nutshell, FRP automates the propagation of changes, meaning when some base values change, all values derived from them are automatically updated. This relieves developers from manually updating variables, leading to less error-prone code.

3.6. FRP Libraries and Implementations

Finally, to bring the theory of FRP into practical use, several languages have libraries facilitating the application of FRP principles. For instance, JavaScript has libraries like `RxJS` and `Bacon.js`, Haskell has `Reactive Banana` and `Yampa`, while Elm is a language built from the ground up around FRP principles. These tools may implement FRP differently but largely adhere to its foundational concepts.

Moving forward, as we progressively unpack Functional Reactive

Programming, remember that these concepts serve as a compass, guiding understanding and orientation. The journey into FRP is, in essence, an exploration into how these concepts interrelate, resulting in a coding practice that is not only functionally comprehensive, but inherently edifying - bringing to the developer, a fresh and efficient way of thinking about coding and systems design.

Chapter 4. The Transition: From Traditional to Functional Reactive Programming

The profound evolution of the digital landscape has instigated a transition from traditional programming towards more advanced methodologies like Functional Reactive Programming (FRP). This shift has been influenced by several factors, including the increasing complexity of applications, the need for better manageability of asynchronous data streams, and the thrust on improving user interaction experience. To truly grasp the depth of this transition, it's essential to start from its roots.

4.1. Emergence of Traditional Programming

Traditional programming has its roots in the early days of software development, where programs were primarily driven by inputs provided by users or systems. This procedural form of programming, also known as imperative programming, primarily revolves around 'states' and 'mutations.' A traditional program typically sets the initial state and then uses a sequence of instructions or commands to mutate this state to achieve the desired outcome. Until the advent of more complex applications, this paradigm served developers well.

However, with the advent of distributed systems and programs requiring real-time responses, managing state in large applications became increasingly complicated. Often, imperative programs' state changes are unpredictable, leading to inconsistencies and bugs that are nearly impossible to trace. This inherent weakness led to the search for programming paradigms that could simplify the management of state and the flow of data, and thus, FRP emerged as a frontline contender.

4.2. Birth and Evolution of Functional Reactive Programming

FRP was first introduced by Conal Elliott and Paul Hudack in 1997 in their paper, "Functional Reactive Animation." Born out of a need to simplify the creation and management of animated and interactive 3D graphics, FRP was initially perceived as a niche construct. However, as applications grew more complex and the Internet era demanded more concurrent and interactive experiences, the core concepts of FRP started gaining traction in broader fields of development.

FRP's philosophy revolves around pure functions and time-varying values known as 'behaviors' and discrete events referred to as 'events.' This shift in perspective from 'state and state changes' to 'data flow and propagation of change' presented an elegant solution to managing stateful computations and asynchronous events.

4.3. Comparing Traditional and Functional Reactive Programming

To understand this transition's profound depth, we can draw some comparisons between traditional programming and FRP.

1. State Management: In traditional programming, state changes are made explicitly by the programmer and can be unpredictable, leading to bugs and inconsistencies. On the other hand, FRP's programming model revolves around the concept of a data flow graph. State changes are propagated automatically through the data flow graphs, making state management easier.

2. Time: In imperative programming, the system's state is typically mutated over time, which can lead to difficult maintenance and debugging issues. FRP introduces time as a primitive aspect of programming, replacing mutable states with time-varying values, offering a more declarative way of handling dynamic behavior.

3. Handling Asynchronous Events: Traditional approaches usually employ callbacks, polling or message passing techniques to handle asynchronicity resulting in callback hell or intricate message passing protocols. FRP emphasizes on functional programming concepts to manage asynchronous events, which can significantly contribute to maintainability and readability of code.

4. Concurrency and Synchronization: Concurrency is one of the pain points in traditional programming models, often leading to race conditions and synchronization issues. The FRP model circumvents many of these problems by propagating changes automatically across the data flow graph, eliminating the need for explicit synchronization in many situations.

5. Efficiency: Imperative programs execute commands sequentially and hold onto resources until the entire sequence has been processed. However, FRP's reactive nature automatically releases resources when they're not needed, leading to efficient resource usage and increased performance.

4.4. Advantages and Challenges of FRP

While the transition from traditional programming to functional reactive programming provides several advantages, it is not without its challenges.

The most distinct advantage of FRP is the elevated abstraction level it provides, allowing developers to think in terms of transformations and data flow, which makes code easier to reason about and more manageable. FRP also manages state more naturally and in a structured manner. Its strong time handling mechanisms make FRP an excellent choice for dealing with real-time systems, GUIs, robotics, and other similar fields.

Conversely, the challenges of incorporating FRP stem from it being a paradigm shift in programming. It demands developers to alter their way of viewing problems, focusing on effects and data flows rather than procedural steps. Additionally, the technical jargon associated with FRP can be a barrier, making it imperative to communicate the FRP concepts effectively. Lastly, given its relatively new stature, the tooling available for FRP is still developing, meaning developers need to build an array of debugging, testing, and validation tools from scratch.

In conclusion, the journey from traditional programming to functional reactive programming epitomizes how mainstream programming has evolved to handle the increasing complexity and diversity of today's software applications. With its promise of simplified data and state management and an intuitive handling of asynchronous operations, FRP is a crucial tool for modern software development. This paradigm's transition does not simply represent an evolutionary step in programming; it is at the very heart of how developers confront and reason their work with increasing complexity and interactivity in contemporary computing environments.

Chapter 5. Understanding the Principles of FRP

Functional Reactive Programming (FRP) is a programming paradigm that has been steadily gaining increased attention over the past decade. Thanks to the complex requirements of modern software systems, popularity for programming methods that can effectively manage complex data flows, interactivity, state management and asynchronous programming has grown greatly.

5.1. Definition and Origin

FRP is a programming paradigm that primarily aims to simplify these issues. It was first introduced in 1997 by Conal Elliott and Paul Hudak in the context of animation and signal processing, but its agnostic principles make it widely applicable. At its core, FRP is a method that combines elements of functional programming (FP) and reactive programming. As a hybrid, FRP is a declarative programming paradigm - meaning code describes what to do, not how to do it - centered around the idea of data flow and change propagation.

5.2. The Basics of FRP: Behaviors and Events

The two primary building blocks of Functional Reactive Programming are Behaviors and Events. Behaviors represent values over time; they're like variables in object-oriented programming, but can change over time. Events, on the other hand, are discrete and represent a value at a specific point in time. Together, they encapsulate the notion of time, and provide a robust and clear way to handle change.

An example would be a mouse pointer on a computer screen as a Behavior, moving fluidly across various positions over time, while clicks of the mouse would be Events, occurring at specific moments in time.

5.3. Mathematics and Semantic Model

To formalize this understanding, FRP is underpinned by a semantic model that describes the notion of time, and combines principles from both continuous and discrete models. The mathematical underpinning of FRP provides reasoning tools that eliminate a whole class of timing bugs and aids in structuring and modularizing time-based, reactive code.

5.4. Asynchronicity and Concurrency

One of the powerful aspects of FRP is its innate ability to handle asynchronicity and concurrency seamlessly. By encapsulating changes in Behaviors and Events, FRP allows for the modeling of complex interactions in a simple and understandable way. This drives away from the typical, and often complicated, callback or promise-based models that can lead to what's commonly called "callback hell".

5.5. Abstraction and Composability

Functional Reactive Programming excels in its ability to create abstract patterns that can be easily composed and reused. This directly results from its roots in functional programming, which emphasizes immutability, side-effect free functions, and higher-order functions. Essentially, within FRP, developers can create a new behavior by applying a function to an existing one creating a whole new layer of abstraction and meaning in a very easy and clear manner.

5.6. The Time Paradigm

In practice, the time-dependence of Behaviors separates FRP from traditional functional languages. This is where the 'reactive' part really takes the spotlight. In an FRP system, changes to Behaviors are propagated throughout the system, enabling automatic and well-defined updates. This forms the basis on which interactive systems, animation, robotics, and other time-dependant computations can be constructed.

5.7. Common Misconceptions

One of the common misconceptions about FRP is the belief that it fits only for UI or front-end development. While much of the demonstrations and applications of FRP have been in the realm of interactive UIs, the principles of FRP are applicable in any situation that involves complex data flows and state management.

That said, it's worth noting that adopting an FRP approach can require a significant shift in how one conceives and designs solutions. It isn't a magic bullet, but, when applied properly, it can lead to far more maintainable and modular code, and ultimately to more robust systems.

In conclusion, Functional Reactive Programming offers a refreshing approach to tackling complexity by providing a model that integrates time flow and composability. By incorporating the best elements of functional programming and reactive programming, FRP offers the potential to significantly modernize the way that complex systems are undertaken. It is much more than a trend - it can be seen as the beginning of a revolution in the way programmers conceive of and structure their code. The details may seem daunting, but the potential benefits suggest FRP is worth a closer look for anyone involved in software development.

Chapter 6. Key Benefits of Adopting FRP

Functional Reactive Programming (FRP) is prized for several reasons; ranging from enhanced code readability to increased system autonomy, there are diverse advantages to adopting this programming paradigm. By leveraging the powerful concepts of reactivity and functional programming principles, we can effectively address a wide array of issues that tend to surface during software development.

6.1. Improved Code Readability and Maintainability

The first significant benefit to adopting FRP is noticeable in the code itself: it becomes more readable, expressive, and maintainable. Since functional reactive programs describe the relationship between system variables over time, the code tends to express high-level behavior concisely. As a consequence, FRP can dramatically reduce code size, easing the burdens of reading, maintaining, and debugging the software.

In the FRP paradigm, programs are built using pure function compositions, limiting side effects and mutations. The states despatched by inputs at any given time are isolated, fostering a clean, easy-to-understand code environment.

Additionally, it's important to recognize FRP's tendency to promote cleaner code organization. Leveraging the time-varied values of behaviors and discrete event sequences of the event stream help to keep parts of the program separate yet easily connectable. This strategic organization can reduce complexity and improve the overall architecture of the system.

6.2. Handling Asynchronous Data Streams

The concept of handling asynchronous data underpins many contemporary applications. Conventional programming models often struggle with this task, leading to tangled logic and erratic system behavior. FRP's fundamental concept of time-varying data stream handling offers a nimble solution.

A predominant number of operations in today's applications, ranging from user interactions, web requests, system notifications to message queues, can be modeled as asynchronous data streams. With FRP, these can be captured concisely and manipulated using a rich set of operators. The end-product is code that straightforwardly and elegantly models complex asynchronous behaviors.

6.3. Decrease in Memory Leaks

Adopting FRP can help reduce memory leaks, a common concern in event-based systems. Traditional systems reliant on callback patterns can inadvertently retain memory, leading to leaks over time; however, FRP allows developers to manage resources more effectively.

Given the architecture of FRP, it employs principles akin to automatic garbage collection to manage resources. When events cease to happen, the corresponding computation and memory allocation are independently dropped. This process frees developers from worrying about memory clean-up after each function, which in turn can go a long way in preventing potential sources of memory leaks.

6.4. Scalability and Performance

FRP is reputably synonymous with superior scalability and

performance. Its inherent adherence to immutability and stateless computations allows it to be flawlessly distributed across different cores or threads, which essentially endorses concurrent processing. This clarity allows potential for parallelism, which is often the path to speed and improved performance on modern multicore processors.

Furthermore, with FRP, we can leverage lazy evaluation, meaning computations are deferred until necessary. This characteristic can boost program efficiency and is especially useful when dealing with extensive data sets or performance-critical paths.

6.5. Testability and Debuggability

Another intriguing advantage of adopting FRP is the augmented testability and debuggability it offers. FRP simplifies the way we reason about code since it encapsulates events and data streams, providing developers a higher level of control. Bearing a declarative nature, it permits us to focus more on the 'what' rather than the 'how,' making debugging tasks easier and more intuitive.

Testing is similarly enhanced under FRP. As data flow is asynchronous and push-based, each event becomes easily testable as it maintains independence from its sources. We can test different sequences of events and their impact on the system without the need for mocking, making the testing process simpler and more accurate.

Regardless of which programming language you're working with or the sector you're working in, considering adopting the FRP paradigm carries significant benefits. It presents a clear path for navigating asynchronous behavior, building scalable systems, and facilitating more manageable, less error-prone codebases. In a climate where technological progress hinges on the quality of software, the time spent understanding and implementing FRP could well be a wise investment.

From readability to debuggability, memory management to scaling, it's clear that FRP offers distinctive advantages. By advancing our programming toolkits with functional reactive principles, we can craft software that's better equipped to meet present and emerging demands. It's more than a paradigm shift; it's a strong step towards future-proof programming.

Chapter 7. Case Studies: Where FRP Shines

FRP is not just an abstract notion; its potential and impact can be truly appraised when put into practical use. To fully comprehend its prowess, let's analyze some case studies where FRP shines the brightest.

7.1. Harnessing Real-time Changes: Interactive Applications

Consider the creation of an interactive application, such as a live data monitoring dashboard. In traditional procedural programming, managing state changes and data flow can become untidy, leading to problematic debugging and, eventually, inefficient performance. Moreover, the synchronous nature of traditional programming could result in blocking of the main thread, thereby lagging the UI updates.

In contrast, FRP's asynchronous and non-blocking nature becomes its greatest strength. It exemplifies the concept of time-varying values and allows for efficient management of state changes.

```
from reactive import Stream

# Stream of data
data_stream = Stream()

# Function to update UI
def update_ui(data):
    pass # Updating UI code here

# Feeding data and notifying UI
for data in live_data_feed:
```

```
    data_stream.notify(data)
    update_ui(data_stream.value)
--------
```

This example demonstrates how a reactive data stream handles real-time data feed. As the data source pushes new data into the stream, the UI function is notified about the change and updates automatically, while maintaining a smooth user experience.

=== Mapping Complex User Interactions: Video Games

Interactive video games are an intricate ensemble of user inputs (buttons, joysticks), AI responses, and continuous graphics rendering. Simulating this interaction using procedural programming might spiral into unmanageable and convoluted code structure, due to nested callbacks and event handlers.

FRP simplifies such complex interaction systems. By treating user inputs and AI responses as data streams, it can manage multitudes of changes efficiently.

[source, javascript]

```javascript
import { merge } from 'most'

const user_action = createStream()

const ai_action = createStream()

const game_stream = merge(user_action, ai_action)

function render_graphics(data) { pass // Graphics rendering code here }
```

game_stream.subscribe({ next: render_graphics, error: error ⇒ console.error(error), complete: () ⇒ console.log('Game Over'), })

By encapsulating user and AI actions in separate streams, and then merging them into a single stream, we achieve a unified, smooth, and manageable data flow. As actions occur, the graphics rendering function is triggered, ensuring real-time updates without blocking.

=== Managing Distributed Systems: Microservices

Microservices architecture is commonly employed in distributed systems for its scalability and resilience. However, monitoring and managing inter-service communication can be cost-intensive and challenging. Event-driven FRP can be a game-changer here.

[source, java]

```java
import io.reactivex.rxjava3.core.Observable;

public class ServiceA {
  private final Subject<String> requestStream =
PublishSubject.create();

  public void sendRequest(String data) {
    requestStream.onNext(data);
  }

  public Observable<String> getRequestStream() {
    return requestStream;
  }
}

public class ServiceB {
  private final ServiceA serviceA;
```

```
  public ServiceB(ServiceA serviceA) {
    this.serviceA = serviceA;

serviceA.getRequestStream().subscribe(this::processReque
st);
  }

  private void processRequest(String data) {
    System.out.println("Processing " + data);
  }
}
```

Here, we model a simple communication between two independent services - ServiceA and ServiceB, using FRP. ServiceA sends requests to ServiceB and ServiceB listens and responds accordingly.

These case studies reiterate FRP's effectiveness in managing asynchronous data streams and complex interactions - a marked shift from callback-based and procedural programming paradigms. As reflected, FRP's approach to time-varying data offers frictionless data flow, simplified error handling, and an overhauled approach to state management. It's crucial to delve deeper into FRP, not just to understand its potential, but to grasp the value it adds to modern software development.

Chapter 8. Challenges and Misconceptions Surrounding FRP

As an emergent paradigm, Functional Reactive Programming (FRP) comes attached with a set of unique challenges and misconceptions. In this extensive analysis, we shall dissect and seek to understand these aspects.

8.1. Understanding FRP's Complexity

One of the notable challenges in adopting FRP is understanding its inherent complexity. It merges the concepts of reactive programming with functional programming, which can be a bit daunting for programmers who are not familiar with either or both. To make matters more challenging, presentations of FRP tend to emphasize its potential for cleaning up clunky asynchronous code, often glossing over the fact that it requires a deep understanding of event streams, signals, behaviors, and a number of higher-order functions. This complexity can make it difficult for new adopters to quickly become productive with FRP.

For those unfamiliar, functional programming is a paradigm that prefers immutability and statelessness. It emphasizes the use of pure functions that eschew side effects. Reactive programming, on the other hand, is all about data streams and the propagation of changes. It allows a developer to create data streams of anything, including variables, user inputs, properties, caches, etc., and react to changes on these

These unique, yet relatively complex concepts make FRP a

challenging landscape for many programmers. This level of complexity often leads individuals to misunderstand and misuse the paradigm, resulting in code that is less efficient than it could be.

8.2. Managing Debugging Challenges

FRP's push-based model means that it can be hard to trace how data is flowing through your program. Systems based on FRP can at times exhibit non-local behavior, which makes it difficult to understand a program's control flow and thus harder to debug.

This is starkly different from the common pull-based models found in most imperative languages, where you request data when you need it rather than reacting to changes. With FRP, debugging can quickly become a game of tracking changes in data across different components of your system, and tying that back to some user action or other event.

Addressing these challenges requires deliberate and careful application of FRP concepts. Exploring new toolsets and debugging strategies, including partial traces, event logging, or adopting FRP library features aimed at debugging, can provide a measure of relief.

8.3. Misconception: FRP as a Silver Bullet

Countless misconceptions abound about FRP, but one of the most common – and damaging – is the belief that FRP is a silver bullet, a magical solution that will resolve all problems and streamline all coding tasks.

Like all paradigms, FRP has its place. It's useful for handling complex, asynchronous tasks involving multiple event sources. However, it might not be the best solution for case-specific, synchronous, or easily sequenced tasks. Believing that FRP is a catch-all solution can lead to inappropriate applications of the paradigm, which can undermine the performance or readability of the code.

8.4. Misconception: FRP Eliminates Bugs and Errors

Another misconception often heard in programming circles is that by adopting FRP, a codebase will instantly become more robust, or even bug-free. In reality, while certain kinds of bugs can become less likely – particularly ones involving inconsistent state – new kinds of bugs can certainly appear.

One common example in FRP is a space leak. This happens when an application retains memory that it no longer needs, primarily because it has to retain information about all past events to manage future ones. This type of leak may occur if the programmer handles the event streams carelessly.

8.5. Misconception: FRP is Equal to Other Paradigms

FRP is also often compared to and mistaken for other paradigms, like reactive programming and stream processing. Reactive programming, as one constituent part of FRP, focuses on asynchronous data streams and the propagation of change, but does not necessarily incorporate the functional approach of function purity and no mutation of state.

Stream processing, on the other hand, shares similar traits with FRP in terms of continuous input streams and queries, but lacks the reactive part where changes propagate through data streams automatically.

In conclusion, while FRP stands as a compelling paradigm, its application is not without challenges and misconceptions. Developers must understand that every paradigm has its respective use cases, and adopting FRP needs careful consideration. It is of utmost importance to dissect and comprehend the intricacies of Functional Reactive Programming before embarking on the journey to adopt it.

In our upcoming chapters, more about functional reactive programming's effective application, unraveling real-life use-cases, and exciting characteristics will be discussed. Let the exploration delve deeper, as the understanding of FRP continues to unfold. The essence of this exploration is not just to learn but to apply knowledge effectively in the ever-evolving landscape of software programming.

Chapter 9. FRP's Role in Modern Software Development

Functional Reactive Programming (FRP) is not only an alternative paradigm for developing software applications; it is also an important tool aiding in the modernization of software development practice. This reactive model contributes to making software applications more robust, responsive, and easier to maintain, proving its worth in the modern landscape.

===FRP Basics

FRP is a unique blend of functional and reactive paradigms in programming. It treats a set of computational operations like a live circuit of data and events that react dynamically to changes over time and user interaction. It takes the advantage of functional programming's immutability and statelessness with reactive's asynchronous data streams, providing a perfect blend for modern solutions.

FRP involves creating, managing, and linking data streams. These streams are sequences of events spread over time that can be manipulated through various functional methods. The ability to combine functional and reactive characteristics can make FRP an essential tool in software development.

9.1. Emphasizing Asynchronicity

Asynchronicity is at the heart of FRP. Modern software systems often have to deal with different kinds of user interactions, network requests, and other operations concurrently. FRP provides a way to write asynchronous and non-blocking code, which can significantly improve the performance and responsiveness of a software system.

Thanks to its asynchronous nature, FRP can help developers effectively manage and balance server-side loads, making software applications more resilient and efficient. With asynchronous actions, developers can compartmentalize processes, leading to improved response times and user experience.

9.2. Handling Complexity

One of the substantial challenges modern software development faces is handling complexity. As applications grow and evolve, their codebase can become difficult to understand, debug, and maintain.

FRP introduces a more declarative coding style, where developers express what to do rather than how to do it. This manifest can improve the readability of the source code, making it more manageable and easier to grasp its functionality. Additionally, stateless nature of functional programming minimizes side effects, allowing developers to isolate and solve problems more effectively.

9.3. FRP in User Interfaces

In terms of building user interfaces (UI), FRP can help manage dynamic content more intuitively. With changes over time identified as a core abstraction in FRP, it brings a whole new fluidity to UI development.

Take, for example, a typical web application. There are input fields, buttons, and other UI elements that cause events (like clicking or typing). With FRP, these events can be handled as streams, responding and updating the UI based on the changes in these streams. This approach allows the process to be more organized and manageable, especially with complicated UIs with numerous interactive elements.

In this regard, FRP brings an invaluable impact on modern web and mobile UI development, where interactive and dynamic content are integral.

9.4. Testing and Debugging Real-Time Systems

Testing and debugging have always been important parts of software development. FRP, with its explicit handling of time and events, can make troubleshooting easier and more predictable.

Thanks to its explicit chronology model, FRP allows developers to simulate and manipulate time in their tests, making it easier to reproduce and discover bugs in the software application. This characteristic can be especially useful when testing real-time systems and dynamic behavior.

9.5. The Influence on Community

Functional Reactive Programming's influence extends beyond just its technical benefits; it has brought about a philosophical change in the development community. Software developers now engage in discussions of a more declarative, expressive programming style and explore how best to handle data streams.

In essence, FRP has helped build a community focused on better, more effective ways to handle complex, real-time software challenges.

9.6. FRP's Adoptability

Although FRP can significantly aid modern software development, its adoption can come with a steep learning curve. Developers accustomed to an imperative style might find the switch challenging due to FRP's distinct paradigm. However, the paradigm's effectiveness in managing complex data streams and handling asynchronicity make it a useful investment.

In closing, the role of Functional Reactive Programming in modern software development cannot be overstated. It provides a powerful set of tools to deal with asynchronicity, manage complexity, and bring more organization to code. From structuring UIs to testing real-time systems, FRP offers solutions tailored to the modern software landscape. Despite the learning curve, embracing this paradigm yields fruitful dividends — a more robust, responsive, and maintainable software application.

Chapter 10. Practical Guide: Implementing FRP in Your Next Project

10.1. Exploring the Basics

FRP is a programming paradigm focused on the manipulation and combination of time-varying data flows. Endowed with the favorable properties of functional programming, it promotes code that is easier to understand and maintain. Further, the concept of 'reactivity' extends functional programming by providing a framework to represent and manipulate computations that vary over time.

To implement FRP in your next project, we'll begin by exploring its key components - Observables and Observers.

Observables generate sequences or 'streams' of events or data over time. Observers, on the other hand, listen and react to these streams. Connecting an Observer to an Observable creates a subscription. This framework enables you to structure your code around reaction to stimuli and data flow, creating a declarative, easily understandable codebase.

10.2. Setting up the Environment

Most modern languages have libraries available to adopt the FRP paradigm. Javascript has popular libraries such as RxJS or Bacon.js, while Scala and Java developers can use libraries like Reactor or Akka Streams. In this guide, we'll conduct our exploration via RxJS, but the general principles carry across languages and libraries.

First, set up your environment. If you're coding in Javascript, initialize a new node project in your CLI:

```
npm init -y
```

Next, install RxJS:

```
npm install rxjs --save
```

This procedure sets the stage to start implementing FRP.

10.3. Creating Your First Observable

It all starts with creating an Observable. In the RxJS context, an Observable is a function that sets up observation. Here is an example:

```
const { Observable } = require('rxjs');

const observable = new Observable(subscriber => {
    subscriber.next(1);
    subscriber.next(2);
    subscriber.next(3);
    setTimeout(() => {
        subscriber.next(4);
        subscriber.complete();
    }, 1000);
});
```

In this example, the Observable emits three immediate values, then a fourth value after one second, then completes.

10.4. Subscribing to an Observable

To invoke the Observable, you must subscribe to it:

```
observable.subscribe({
    next(x) { console.log('Value: ' + x); },
    error(err) { console.error('Error: ' + err); },
    complete() { console.log('Completed'); }
});
```

Function hooks - 'next', 'error', and 'complete' - are provided to the Observable during subscription, setting responses to different events. Here, each new value is logged, errors are caught, and completion is indicated.

10.5. Sharing an Observable

In some cases, you'll want several observers to share a single execution of an Observable. Here the share() operator comes to the rescue:

```
const { share } = require('rxjs/operators');

const shared = observable.pipe(share());
```

10.6. Error Handling in FRP

Error handling is a crucial part of any programming endeavor. With Observables, error handling is streamlined:

```
observable.subscribe({
    next(x) { throw 'Error!'; },
```

```
        error(err) { console.error('Caught: ' + err); }
});
```

Even if an error is thrown in the 'next' function, it is caught and passed to the 'error' function of the subscriber, ensuring that unexpected crashes are avoidable.

10.7. Unsubscribing from Observables

Observables retain resources as long as there's a subscriber receiving their output. To release these resources, one must unsubscribe:

```
const subscription = observable.subscribe({...});
subscription.unsubscribe();
```

10.8. Transforming Streams

The power of FRP comes from the ability to manipulate data streams effortlessly. For this, a gamut of operators like map, filter, reduce, and scan are available:

```
const { map } = require('rxjs/operators');

observable
    .pipe(map(value => value * 2))
    .subscribe(console.log);  //prints 2, 4, 6, 8
```

Here, the map operator multiplies each value by two before it is sent to the subscriber.

10.9. Combining Streams

The robust `zip`, `combineLatest`, `withLatestFrom`, and `merge` operators help to combine streams:

```
const { from, zip } = require('rxjs');
const { map } = require('rxjs/operators');

const streamA = from([1, 2, 3]);
const streamB = from([4, 5, 6]);
const combined = zip(streamA, streamB);

combined.subscribe(console.log);  //prints [1,4], [2,5],
[3,6]
```

In the above example, values from `streamA` and `streamB` are paired up and emitted as an array.

Closing Remarks

Functional Reactive Programming inculcates an exciting development approach based on time-varying data flows. Through this practical guide, your voyage into the world of FRP should be smoother, and you should now be geared to bring the power of FRP to your upcoming projects. Always remember that FRP involves a learning curve and is a continual process. Don't be frightened to experiment and make mistakes. Embrace FRP wholeheartedly, and witness the revolution that it brings to your programming prowess.

Chapter 11. Looking Forward: The Future of Functional Reactive Programming

As we gaze into the glass ball of the future, observing the scenic trajectory of Functional Reactive Programming (FRP), there's little doubt that this paradigm occupies an influential place in both currently emerging and future software designs. With its applicability in a broad spectrum of areas - from enhancing the user experience in web applications to offering sturdy, error-free protocols in backend development, FRP is maturing from a theoretical construct into a practical tool. Here's how we see it.

11.1. The Implication of FRP on Web Development

Web development, especially interactive and real-time user interfaces, is an area ripe for the influence of FRP. FRP's core feature of dealing with dynamic data flows in a principled manner provides its primary value here. Developers increasingly encounter situations where they need to manage multiple asynchronous data streams and reactive updates for a more responsive and engaging user experience. Here, FRP's features replicate the async-await syntax—promises in JavaScript, for instance—making the code more readable and easier to debug.

As technology evolves, so does the complexity of user interactions. From single clicks to swipes, from simple forms to layered user input sequences, monitoring user behavior on websites is becoming increasingly complex. FRP can encode these complex interactions as first-class reactive entities that are no less tractable than 'onClick' events.

11.2. Benefiting Backend Development

On the server-side, backends are manifesting an increase in the frequency of communication. An application often involves multiple components communicating simultaneously and responding to each other's updates. Traditional request-response models and callback-based design are harder to manage as the system complexity increases. FRP offers an effective solution by encapsulating these interactions into functional units that react to updates. This ability makes applications more robust and maintainable while dealing with multi-threading and multi-service architectures.

11.3. Modernizing Legacy Systems

When it comes to rejuvenating legacy systems, the functional approach inherent in FRP could serve as a mighty ally. It encourages developers to divide monolithic systems into independently functional modules. This modularization can give companies access to legacy system data that wasn't previously available, and developers can iteratively improve and replace legacy system modules without risking a complete system overhaul.

11.4. FRP and Distributed Systems

FRP is especially relevant in distributed systems, where dealing with data flows is endemic. Distributed systems grapple with issues of event ordering, data propagation, and buffering—all features encapsulated in the core FRP model. Having these features incorporated as part of the dataflow model simplifies the management of such distributed systems.

11.5. FRP in Data Streaming and Big Data

Related to the Internet of Things (IoT) and Big Data, FRP provides an inherent advantage of querying, transforming, and aggregating data on the fly. Think about real-time analytics, predictive analytics, or real-time decision making. In all these cases, FRP's dataflow paradigm is a natural fit—data naturally flows from one transformation to the next, providing a continuous stream.

11.6. FRP in Cyber-Physical Systems

Cyber-physical systems (CPS), which imply a tight conjoining of and coordination between the system's computational and physical elements, find an attractive proposition in the FRP paradigm. Applications like robotics, autonomous vehicles, and power management systems can benefit from the fluid modality ensured by FRP, where response times can significantly improve, and operations become more reliable.

11.7. Evolution of FRP Language and Tools

While FRP's benefits are notable, there exist a series of challenges to widespread adoption. The application of FRP concepts isn't always straightforward, leading to cases of misuse or overcomplication. However, with the continual evolution of tooling and language features that simplify FRP for the everyday developer, this trend is changing.

Modern languages and frameworks are starting to incorporate FRP or similar paradigms to make it more probable that they'll effectively be used in production environments. For example, JavaScript has

RxJS, Java has Reactor, and Python has RxPY. Modern FRP libraries like these will undoubtedly lower the barrier of entry and encourage wider adoption among developers.

Future language advancements may further drive the adoption of FRP by incorporating built-in support or driving FRP principles at a lower level in the execution model. There's potential for FRP to become a standard feature in programming languages, with first-class support.

11.8. FRP and AI: A Progressive Partnership

In the realm of Artificial Intelligence (AI) and Machine Learning (ML), FRP finds a lot of promising applications. These systems often involve the processing of real-time data streams for analysis and decision making. The processing pipeline in these systems closely maps to a dataflow model, making FRP a fitting paradigm. Furthermore, AI and ML's dependency on scalable computational models is an area where the FRP paradigm can particularly shine.

In conclusion, Functional Reactive Programming carries a momentum that can't be ignored. As developers seek out ways to overcome the challenges posed by increasingly complex system interactions and demands in fields like IoT, Big Data, and AI, FRP is well-poised to enhance productivity and efficaciousness in programming. Therefore, making sense of this paradigm and its applications is more than an academic exercise—it's a pragmatic preparation for the road ahead.

www.ingramcontent.com/pod-product-compliance
Lightning Source LLC
LaVergne TN
LVHW051625050326

832903LV00033B/4659